BY HIS
Grace
FOR HIS
Glory

AN INDUCTIVE BIBLE STUDY
ON THE BOOK OF ROMANS

By
Erin H. Warren

contents

start here

I love Romans. It's foundational yet deep. It's simple yet complex. It is an incredibly powerful book that has been changing lives for centuries. In the fourth century, St. Augustine, one of the great theologians, was far from God. But then he read Romans 13. Those verses stirred conviction and removed all doubt. He put his faith in Jesus, and the Church was changed forever by his ministry. In the 1500s, while translating the Bible in German, Martin Luther read Romans 1:17. It completely changed his view of the Gospel and of faith, leading to the Protestant Reformation. In the eighteenth century, John Wesley heard a reading of Martin Luther's commentary on Romans and it ignited his faith. A revival in England followed. The words in these sixteen chapters have the power to change our faith too . . . if we let them.

There are many familiar verses in Romans, and we associate this book with the Gospel and evangelism. But it is so much more! In fact, William Tyndale in his preface to the book of Romans says this:

> *Forasmuch as this epistle is the principal and most excellent part of the new Testament and most pure evangelion, that is to say glad tidings, and that we call gospel, and also is a light and a way unto the whole scripture; I think it meet that every christian man not only know it, by rote and without the book, but also exercise himself therein evermore continually, as with the daily bread of the soul. No man verily can read it too oft, or study it too well; for the more it is studied, the easier it is; the more it is chewed, the pleasanter it is; and the more groundly it is searched, the preciouser things are found in it, so great treasure of spiritual things lieth hid therein.*[1]

The book of Romans is essential to understanding the Gospel. It is like a mirror, beckoning us to see ourselves in the True Light. It reminds us of who we are, what Jesus did, why He did it, and what we now have because of it. It's more than a list of dos and don'ts or the way we are saved, it's a letter that reveals the character of our Way Maker God, the One who bends down to His people, who longs to see everyone find hope in Him. It's the good news that we need each and every day of our lives, and we will never reach an end to the treasures that await us in this powerful letter. Everything we have and all that we are is by His grace for His glory.

---

1   *Doctrinal Treatises and Introductions to Different Portions of the Holy Scriptures* by William Tyndale, Henry Walter, ed. [Cambridge: University Press, 1848], p 484

A LITTLE BACKGROUND INFORMATION

The letter to the Romans was written by the Apostle Paul in the late 50s AD (most likely around 57 AD). He wrote this letter to the church in Rome, a church he had not even visited before (though he expresses his desire to do so). This church was a mix of both Jewish and Gentile (non-Jewish) believers, and there was turmoil within the church over their differences. About a decade earlier, Emperor Claudius expelled all Jews from Rome (see Acts 18:2). About five years later, when Emperor Claudius died, the edict was repealed, and some Jewish Christians returned to Rome to find a primarily Gentile church. The Jews and Gentiles were arguing over cultural aspects in the practice of their faith: the Law, circumcision, Sabbath, and their freedom in Christ. Paul desired to see a unified church in Rome, and I'd argue that one of his main themes throughout this letter is unity in diversity with the purpose of glorifying God together. We are all common in our sin and common in our salvation. In this, his longest letter, Paul speaks to their cultural differences and resets the foundation of their faith and what matters. The letter can be divided into four sections:

Chapters 1-4: God's Righteousness vs. Our Need for a Savior
Chapters 5-8: Our Lives Because of the Gospel
Chapters 9-11: Fulfillment of God's Old Testament Promises
Chapters 12-16: Practical Advice

One quick note: Romans is a hard book to swallow at times, but especially in the first two and a half chapters. This is why it's so important to keep the historical context top of mind as we study. It's easy to beat ourselves up, to feel like we are the scum of the earth while reading the first couple of chapters, but I challenge to you press through. In order to fully understand our salvation, we must understand why we need a Savior and what we have been saved from. This is why the book of Romans is so foundational to our faith. Don't give up! Press on and endure through these hard passages. I promise you: it's worth it.

WHY STUDY INDUCTIVELY?

Several years ago, I was sitting in my seat at a women's conference, expectant and ready to hear from God. This quote from one of my favorite Bible teachers forever changed my perspective on the Word of God:

We cannot be content being curators of other people's opinions about a book we cannot be bothered to read ourselves. — Jen Wilkin

That was the lightbulb moment when I realized what was missing: personal study of God's Word. I had merely been a librarian, curating other people's study findings and revelations. I had never learned to study God's Word for myself. There are a myriad of reasons why we don't study His Word firsthand: too busy, not equipped with the right tools, misinformation about women and the Bible. I could go on and on, but I think if we truly knew the power that the Word of God has in our lives, we wouldn't be able to put it down.

It became my passion to equip and encourage women to study Scripture for themselves. When I began to study this way, I found my life changing. I found I was memorizing Scripture, remembering His character, and overcoming in ways I never had before. And can I let you in on a little secret? It was *way* easier than I ever expected.

This way of studying is called "inductive" Bible study, but that can be an intimidating word. It simply means studying with your own heart and mind first, trusting the Holy Spirit to do what He promises to do (John 14:26), before turning to other sources. It's learning to ask the right questions of Scripture and to read through a God-centered lens (more on this in a moment) versus a me-centered lens.

I designed this study to help you do just that: to pull out the details, to see the character of God and ask the right questions of the passage. It's not your typical study book. I won't lead you, but instead walk alongside you and guide you as you discover the truths in Romans for yourself. My heart and goal for Feasting on Truth and these studies is to help you:

- Release the bonds of a "perfect quiet time" to find deeper, richer time in the Word

- Build confidence as you learn how to study the Bible firsthand

- Discover truths about God and His character

- Connect the Old and New Testaments

- Grow in your faith and knowledge in a way that produces life change

HOW TO USE THIS STUDY

Feasting on Truth has several levels of studies, and I classify this one as True Inductive. We will use four simple questions (see page 9) to guide our study. Each week will focus on one chapter, and you'll see that the homework includes a guide through those four questions. Under *What Does This Mean?* you'll see some suggested words to look up in the dictionary as well as space to write cross-references (other verses that speak to the same topic or help explain the meaning). There are also some starter questions to help kick-start your study but won't cover everything. These are intended to help get you thinking on your own and are not all-inclusive of the meaning.

I purposely left this section wide open for you, or rather for the Holy Spirit. I want you to have the freedom to take notes in the format you choose: write out specific verses, record observations, make a chart, rewrite commentary quotes or Greek definitions, etc. Each week also includes pages for teaching notes and group notes. I know it can sound intimidating, but I also know you can do it!

Teaching for each chapter is available on Season 9 of the Feasting on Truth Podcast or my YouTube channel: www.FeastingOnTruth.com/c/erinhwarren.

Here are some more tips to help you as you study:

Move Slowly

Many Bible studies plow through Scripture, covering a chapter (or sometimes more) a day. There's certainly a time and a place for that, but I've found when I move through Scripture slowly, reading small sections or focusing on one aspect of the study over the course of one week, the Word of God soaks into my heart and mind deeply. I remember it more easily. I memorize it more effectively. What I love about this particular way of studying is that if I feel the need to stop and let a particular verse sink in, I can do so without feeling like I'm falling behind. It also leaves room for the Holy Spirit to do what only He can do. Which leads me to . . .

Let the Holy Spirit Guide You

In John 14:26, Jesus promises, "But the Helper, the Holy Spirit, whom the Father will send in my name, he will teach you all things and bring to your remembrance all that I have said to you." When I sit down to study, I start with prayer. I ask the Holy Spirit to teach me all the things and to help me remember all the things. That's His job. He's there to help, so invite Him into your time.

Take the Pressure Off

Our time with the Lord doesn't have to be a picture-perfect composition of Bible, notebook, and a cup of coffee (oh how I do love me some good coffee though). The words "quiet time" are not in the Bible; one size does not fit all. Our time in the Word changes with our stage of life. I tend to deep-dive study about twice a week, but I meditate on it every day. You may do all of your study in one day or you may devote an hour a day. Find what works for you and stick with it!

Don't Do This Alone

Some of my deepest relationships are ones built on the Word. They are women who gathered around a table or in a living room or online, and we had hard conversations with the Word of Truth between us. Invite a few girlfriends to do this with you. I even included a fun recipe in the back of the book you can make when you get together!

I recommend completing all of the homework on your own before listening to the teaching for the week. You can either listen on your own time or watch together with your group.

Finding time is hard. Women often tell me that they need to put their families first, that work is too crazy, or that they just don't have time to get together with other women for Bible study. Can I challenge you a bit? Is there any time more well spent than investing in our relationship with God? It's hard to pour out from an empty cup. We need to be constantly filled with Jesus, so we can pour out Jesus to our friends, family, and to God. Yes, this may look different in different seasons of life, but you won't regret making it a priority to spend time in the Word with other women.

COMPANION TEACHINGS AND OTHER RESOURCES

I am committed to walking alongside you as you study Scripture inductively. I know you can do this, and I want to help you be successful. I have personally curated and put together a valuable study resource for you called *The Alongside Guide*. Each week, you'll receive an email from me with helpful insight, links to that week's teaching video and podcast, study notes with cross-references, quotes, characteristics of God, small group discussion questions, and more. It's everything you need to be successful in your study, and it gets delivered right to your inbox. Scan the QR code or visit FeastingOnTruth.com/Romans to sign up.

I hope and pray that through the study of Romans, your passion for God's Word will be ignited, that you will crave His Words more than any human's, and that you will grow in your confidence to open your Bible and study on your own.

I am cheering for you and praying for you!

Because of Christ,

Erin H. Warren

four simple questions

Good Bible study is rooted in asking the right questions of Scripture. While this study gives you some specific questions to answer, you can begin to go deeper into understanding the passage by asking four simple questions. Our first inclination is to ask, "What does this mean to me?" We want to cut right to the ending. Instead, learning to first understand the context, summary, and character of God in the passage will help us better discern the meaning and our response. I have adopted what I call *Four Simple Questions* as the foundation of my time in the Word. Yes, this takes a little more time and effort, but the practice of persevering through the Word is a valuable one. These four simple questions, as well as other helpful tips and resources for inductive study, are further explained in my book, *Feasting on Truth: Savor the Life-giving Word of God.*

START WITH CONTEXT

It's important to remember that while the Bible was written for us and is applicable to our lives today (Hebrews 4:12), we are not the original audience. It is a book not written in modern America, but in the ancient Middle East. If we do not first answer some key questions to understand the context, we cannot properly understand the passage and its intent. Most of these answers can be found in a good study Bible.

FOUR SIMPLE QUESTIONS

I realized that one of my downfalls when attempting to read and study the Bible for myself was not knowing which questions to ask. Many of the methods I tried were either too open or too rigid. Asking four simple questions provided the right balance of structure and flexibility I needed. I want to release you from thinking this has to look a certain way—it doesn't. Basically: Are you showing up? Are you changing? Are you connected? Does that make you want to keep showing up? If you answer yes to all of these, then you're on the right track! Here is a brief overview of each question:

1. **What does this say?**

   Before we can interpret Scripture, we need to know what's going on in the passage. Some methods would call this *observation* or the *aim of the passage.*

   - Write a 1–2 sentence summary of what the passage is about—no interpretation, just the facts.

   - Answer the questions: Who? What? Where? When?

   - Are there any repeated words or phrases?

   - Are there any transitional words (therefore, so, but, and, etc.)? Remember, every word is there for a reason.

2. **What does this say about God?**

   This to me has been the most transformative question to ask during Bible study. This book is not about us; it's about God. His character and name are written on every page. Before we can understand our response, we must know who He is.

   - What names of God are used? (His names speak to His character.)

   - What characteristics of God are in this passage?

   - I include Jesus in this as well: What does this passage tell us about Jesus?

   - You can find lists of the names and characteristics of God on pages 16–17.

   - Each week, complete the sentence "Because God is _____, I can _____."

3. **What does this mean?**

   PRAY. PRAY. PRAY. Ask the Holy Spirit to guide you in this. Using context, the summary, and other observations you have made, begin to be a detective. Remember the lens through which you are looking. Yes, this takes work, but it's worth doing!

   - Read the passage in multiple translations. What differences do you see?

   - Look up words in the English dictionary.

   - What other passages in Scripture are related to this one? (These are called cross-references.)

   - Read a trusted commentary or study Bible.

   - Research the original language (the Old Testament was originally written in Hebrew and the New Testament in Greek).

   - Go to FeastingOnTruth.com/Resources for recommended resources, Bibles, and commentaries.

4. **How should I respond?**

   Our Bible study should change us. John 17:17 says, "Sanctify them in the truth; your word is truth." *Sanctify* is a big churchy word that means "to purify or to make holy." It's the act of separating ourselves from the actions of our flesh and dedicating more of our lives and actions to God. God's Word has a purpose in our lives (Isaiah 55:10–11), and we shouldn't stop at knowing its meaning. Instead, we should respond:

   - Is there an action I need to take?

- A conversation I need to have?

- A moment of worship?

- Something I should let go?

- Write out a prayer.

However you feel led to respond, write it down and enlist someone to hold you accountable.

OTHER HELPFUL TIPS

Listen to the Passage

Use a Bible app to listen to the passages each week. We often feel like this is a cop-out, but for thousands of years, the Word of God was passed down orally from generation to generation. It's a book meant to be read out loud, and when you listen to it, you'll be amazed at how much you pick up on that you didn't notice when reading it.

Use Different Colored Pens

I've found using different colored pens when writing my study notes helps me remember where the note came from. For instance, I use different colors for rewriting the Scripture verses, my thoughts, certain study Bibles, cross-references or different translations, commentary quotes, and Greek or Hebrew word definitions. I don't really have a color system, so the colors change from time to time. That's okay too!

Start with a Clean Copy of God's Word

A study Bible adds additional commentary. Using a Bible that doesn't have any additional commentary removes the temptation to peek at notes before fully understanding the passage on your own. If you do not have a non-study Bible, don't fret! You can print out chapters on several Bible websites including www.BibleGateway.com. I use an ESV journaling Bible for my initial study (which has very few footnotes), then move to other versions and other study Bibles as I go through my study week. Speaking of translations . . .

A Note About Translations

There are a myriad of translations out there, so how do you know which to pick? First, it's important to know where translations come from. The Old Testament was originally written in Hebrew, while the New Testament was written in Greek (though a few portions were written in Aramaic).

Over the years, translators have used original copies written in these languages to interpret Scripture into English (and other languages as well). Translations fall on a spectrum between two ends: word-for-word (translations that use the closest English word to the original word) and thought-for-thought (translations that rephrase the words into more modern, understandable English). Technically, all of them are a mix of the two, but some lean more toward one end or the other.

Some examples of translations that lean toward word-for-word include: English Standard Version (ESV—my top choice), New American Standard Bible (NAS or NASB), and King James Version (KJV). These are the closest to the original language, but we can sometimes miss the cultural context.

An example of thought-for-thought is the New Living Translation (NLT).

There are also versions that are more toward the middle of the spectrum, such as the Christian Standard Bible (CSB) and the New International Version (NIV).

The last kind of translation is not necessarily a translation at all, but rather a paraphrase. Paraphrase Bibles, like *The Message*, should be treated more like commentary because, while they can bring insight into the meaning of the passage, they are not Scripture themselves. I rarely use this type. If you do use a paraphrase, wait until you've completed questions 1–3 and are consulting other commentaries for additional insights.

Welcome to the Feast!

See? Simple. Yes, it takes practice, but honestly, it doesn't take as long as you'd think. You just have to be willing to spend time with Jesus. In Acts 4, Peter and John are on trial before the religious leaders (the smartest of the smart when it came to the Law), and in verse 13 it says, "Now when they saw the boldness of Peter and John, and perceived that they were uneducated, common men, they were astonished. And they recognized that they had been with Jesus." Uneducated. Common. Peter and John hadn't been to seminary, but they had been *with* Jesus.

What I've found is that there is not one method that will make all of this work for you. The power is not in the method. The power is in the Word of God. The power is in spending time with Jesus in the Word with the Holy Spirit as your guide.

When you see your life change and you find community around the Word, you will find yourself returning to Scripture, growing more confident as you study, and discovering the joy and excitement of Feasting on Truth.

Visit FeastingOnTruth.com/HowTo for more information
and in-depth teachings on these questions.

small group guide

I am a firm believer in gathering together around the Word of God. It is at the heart of Feasting on Truth. As stated in *start here*, I believe that small group discussion is incredibly important when studying the Bible. I heard a pastor say, "Our time in the Word should be personal but never private." I do not believe we are called to study in isolation, and I believe it is in those places of isolation where Satan loves to tempt us. Discussing the passage in a small group setting (even if it's with only one other woman) helps confirm what the Holy Spirit taught you. It holds us accountable to truth. Not only that, but I learn so much from other women too. They will see truths within those passages that I miss. It helps build layers of understanding.

Leading a group is not nearly as difficult as it seems. I like to think of group leaders more like discussion leaders. A great discussion leader talks less than a third of the group time. You may need to speak first or jump in to get the conversation going, but the goal is to get the group talking.

Teaching for each chapter is available on Season 9 of the Feasting on Truth podcast or my YouTube channel: YouTube.com/c/erinhwarren.

Here are some other tips and a guide for your small group time:

Lead with authenticity

You do not have to have all the answers or have it all together to lead. I do not have it all together, and I fail miserably every day at doing what I know I should (Romans 7!). But I don't have to air all my dirty laundry to be authentic, and I never want my authenticity to enable sin in other people's lives. I've found that when I'm real about where I am and I invite women in to see how God is working on me in those areas, it invites them into authentic life change as well.

Set up a group text or use a group chat app

Connection throughout the week is key to building connection within your group. If you are not tech savvy or keeping up with a group chat isn't your strength, ask someone in the group to take charge of that. It's a great way to get others involved too! Throughout the week, you can check in on your group or share a verse or a particular insight into the passage.

Start with an ice breaker question

It doesn't have to be deep or spiritual, just something to get the conversation flowing. These types of questions are always a great way to help a group of women get to know each other.

Share your summary

Have the women share their summary for that week's passage. Depending on the size of your group, you may want to limit this to two to three women.

Ask: What characteristics of God did you see in this week's passage?

This works well "popcorn style." Let the women jump in with various names and characteristics of God and the verses that correspond. I usually add these to my own notes as well.

Use the weekly discussion questions

There are discussion questions marked within each week's homework. For additional weekly discussion questions, go to FeastingOnTruth.com/Romans and sign up to receive *The Alongside Guide* in your email. Each week, you'll get additional questions (as well as other resources and notes) delivered right to your inbox.

Share "Because God is" statements

This is a simple one, and I love it when everyone shares theirs! Depending on how long you have been together, some women in your group may not feel comfortable sharing the nitty-gritty of their lives. Having everyone share their "Because God is" statement is a way to engage the women who do not feel comfortable speaking up.

Share prayer requests

Sharing what is going on in our lives opens the door to build community and meet needs. I'll never forget sitting in a group when a woman shared that she needed prayer that she could pass her driving test. Across the table, another woman in the group spoke up and said, "I can help you learn to drive!" A couple months later, I received a picture of the two women holding a brand-new driver's license. It was incredible! Praying for one another is commanded, so allow time for this with your group. Pray with one another. Pray throughout the week. When we do this, we get to share an inheritance in what God is doing through the lives of others.

GROUP LIST

NAME	PHONE	EMAIL

knowing God

For too many years, I struggled with knowing how to interpret Scripture and apply these ancient words to my life. I did not know that God promises to equip us in studying Scripture through the Holy Spirit. And truthfully, I treated my Bible like one of those balls you shake, ask a question, flip over, and find your answer. Too many times I came to Scripture looking for an answer to my question, or I treated it like a yearbook—looking for all the pictures of myself.

Then, I began asking a different question, and my entire Bible study and life changed. I asked, "What does this say about God?" This shifted my perspective from a self-centered approach toward Scripture (where I am always asking, "What does this mean *to* me or *for* me?") to a God-centered approach—intentionally looking for and seeking out what each passage teaches me about God.

The Bible is not about me. It is first and foremost a book about God, and His name and character are written across every page. Our purpose on earth is to know God and make Him known, to love God and love others. But we can't love what we don't know; we can't worship what we don't know. And the primary way we know God is through His Word. The pursuit of knowledge about God is not optional; it's essential.

On the following pages, you will find two lists to help you: Names of God and Characteristics of God. It's not comprehensive, and there are spaces for you to add others as you discover more with each passage you read. Here are ways you can have a God-centered approach to your study:

- Ask, "What characteristics of God do I see in this passage?"

- Ask, "What names of God do I see in this passage?" (His names speak to His character.)

- Complete this sentence: Because God is _____, I can _____.

I understand there are different roles of the Trinity (God the Father, God the Son, God the Holy Spirit), but for the sake of simplicity (and especially as you are beginning), I think of them as One. If you need further help, visit www.FeastingOnTruth.com for more information and resources.

names of God

Abba Father

Adonai *(Lord, Master)*

Alpha and Omega

Bread of Life

Chief Cornerstone

Creator

Deliverer

El Elyon *(The Most High God)*

El Olam *(The Everlasting God)*

El Roi *(The God Who Sees Me)*

El Shaddai *(The Lord God Almighty)*

Elohim

Everlasting Father

Great High Priest

Holy One

I AM

Immanuel

King of Kings

Lamb of God

Light of the World

Lion of Judah

Lord of Lords

Mighty God

Morning Star

Prince of Peace

Resurrection and the Life

Savior

Wonderful Counselor

Yahweh Amen *(The Lord is Truth)*

Yahweh Jireh *(The Lord Provides)*

Yahweh Nissi *(The Lord is my Banner)*

Yahweh-Raah *(The Lord is my Shepherd)*

Yahweh Rapha *(The Lord Heals)*

Yahweh Shalom *(The Lord is Peace)*

characteristics of God

Abounding in Steadfast Love

Compassionate

Deliberate

Faithful

Forgiving

Full of Grace

Good

Glorious

Gracious

Guide

Holy

Immutable *(Unchanging)*

Infinite

Invisible

Jealous

Just

Kind

Long-Suffering/Patient

Love

Merciful

Mighty

Omnipotent *(All-Powerful)*

Omnipresent

Omniscient *(All-Knowing)*

One

Perfect

Protector

Provider

Refuge/Help

Righteous

Self-Sufficient

Slow to Anger

Sovereign

Trustworthy

Truth

Wise

With Us

KNOWING GOD NOTES

BY HIS

Grace

FOR HIS

Glory

CONTEXT

CONTEXT NOTES

Who wrote the book of Romans?

What do you know about this author?

To whom was this book written?

When was it written?

What is the genre of this book?

What was the intent or purpose?

What was going on in history when it was written?

CONTEXT NOTES

CONTEXT NOTES

TEACHING NOTES

TEACHING NOTES

GROUP NOTES

GROUP NOTES

By His

Grace

For His

Glory

ROMANS 1

READ ROMANS 1

WHAT DOES THIS SAY?

Write a 2–3 sentence summary of this passage.

Who? What? Where? When?

List any repeated words or phrases.

List any transitional words.

ROMANS 1 NOTES

WHAT DOES THIS SAY ABOUT GOD?

What characteristics of God do you see in this passage?

WHAT DOES THIS MEAN?

Look up the following words in the dictionary and write out their definitions:

Creator:

Honor:

_____:

_____:

ROMANS 1 NOTES

CROSS-REFERENCES

Habakkuk 2:4:

Psalm 19:1–6:

1 Peter 4:1–6:

_____:

_____:

STARTER QUESTIONS

How does Paul describe Jesus?

DISCUSSION: How does Paul describe the gospel?

How do the people respond to God?

DISCUSSION: How does sin suppress truth?

DISCUSSION: How do honor and thanksgiving help us glorify God? What is the risk if we do not give honor or thanks to God?

ROMANS 1 NOTES

HOW SHOULD I RESPOND?

What is the Holy Spirit asking me to do in light of this passage?

Write a prayer of honor and thanksgiving for who God is in this passage.

Because God is:

    I can:

TEACHING NOTES

TEACHING NOTES

GROUP NOTES

GROUP NOTES

BY HIS

Grace

FOR HIS

Glory

ROMANS 2

READ ROMANS 2

WHAT DOES THIS SAY?

Write a 2–3 sentence summary of this passage.

Who? What? Where? When?

List any repeated words or phrases.

List any transitional words.

WHAT DOES THIS SAY ABOUT GOD?

What characteristics of God do you see in this passage?

WHAT DOES THIS MEAN?

Look up the following words in the dictionary and write out their definitions:

Righteous:

Forbear:

_____:

_____:

CROSS-REFERENCES

Proverbs 24:12:

Jeremiah 2:5–10:

Ezekiel 36:20–23:

_____:

_____:

STARTER QUESTIONS

DISCUSSION: How does God's kindness lead to repentance?

Why are we a poor judge?

What role does humility play in our relationship with God?

DISCUSSION: What does Paul say about the outward appearance vs. inward obedience?

ROMANS 2 NOTES

HOW SHOULD I RESPOND?

What is the Holy Spirit asking me to do in light of this passage?

Write a prayer of honor and thanksgiving for who God is in this passage.

Because God is:

    I can:

TEACHING NOTES

TEACHING NOTES

GROUP NOTES

GROUP NOTES

BY HIS
Grace
FOR HIS
Glory

ROMANS 3

READ ROMANS 3

WHAT DOES THIS SAY?

Write a 2–3 sentence summary of this passage.

Who? What? Where? When?

List any repeated words or phrases.

List any transitional words.

WHAT DOES THIS SAY ABOUT GOD?

What characteristics of God do you see in this passage?

WHAT DOES THIS MEAN?

Look up the following words in the dictionary and write out their definitions:

Redemption:

Propitiation:

Faith:

Justified:

_____:

_____:

CROSS-REFERENCES

Leviticus 16:15–19:

Ephesians 2:1–9:

Hebrews 9:11–15:

_____:

_____:

STARTER QUESTIONS

DISCUSSION: Why is the law insufficient to save?

How are we saved?

How do faith and the Law work together?

DISCUSSION: How do these quoted verses help explain this passage?

Psalm 51:4

Psalm 14:1–3

Psalm 53:1–3

Psalm 5:9

Psalm 140:3

Psalm 10:7

Proverbs 1:16

Proverbs 3:15–17

Isaiah 59:7

Psalm 36:1

DISCUSSION: How does the Gospel change the way we approach God?

ROMANS 3 NOTES

ROMANS 3 NOTES

HOW SHOULD I RESPOND?

What is the Holy Spirit asking me to do in light of this passage?

Write a prayer of honor and thanksgiving for who God is in this passage.

Because God is:

    I can:

58

TEACHING NOTES

TEACHING NOTES

GROUP NOTES

GROUP NOTES

By His Grace for His Glory

ROMANS 4

READ ROMANS 4

WHAT DOES THIS SAY?

Write a 2–3 sentence summary of this passage.

Who? What? Where? When?

List any repeated words or phrases.

List any transitional words.

WHAT DOES THIS SAY ABOUT GOD?

What characteristics of God do you see in this passage?

WHAT DOES THIS MEAN?

Look up the following words in the dictionary and write out their definitions:

Grace:

Credited/ Counted:

Hope:

_____:

_____:

CROSS-REFERENCES

Genesis 15:5–6:

Genesis 17:5:

Psalm 32:1–2:

_____:

_____:

STARTER QUESTIONS

What do you know about Abraham? (see Genesis 12–25)

DISCUSSION: Why was it important to note that Abraham was counted as righteous before he was circumcised? Why is that good news for us?

What does it mean to hope "against hope"?

DISCUSSION: Write down some of God's promises from Scripture. How can you continue to call these to mind?

ROMANS 4 NOTES

HOW SHOULD I RESPOND?

What is the Holy Spirit asking me to do in light of this passage?

Write a prayer of honor and thanksgiving for who God is in this passage.

Because God is:

    I can:

TEACHING NOTES

TEACHING NOTES

GROUP NOTES

GROUP NOTES

By His Grace
For His Glory

ROMANS 5

READ ROMANS 5

WHAT DOES THIS SAY?

Write a 2–3 sentence summary of this passage.

Who? What? Where? When?

List any repeated words or phrases.

List any transitional words.

WHAT DOES THIS SAY ABOUT GOD?

What characteristics of God do you see in this passage?

WHAT DOES THIS MEAN?

Look up the following words in the dictionary and write out their definitions:

Endurance/ Perseverance:

Character:

Reconciled:

_____:

_____:

CROSS-REFERENCES

James 1:2–4:

1 Corinthians 15:21–22; 45–49:

_____ :

_____ :

STARTER QUESTIONS

DISCUSSION: What does it mean to have "peace with God"? What benefits does peace provide?

What three things does Paul call us to rejoice in? Why can we rejoice in these?

What do you know about Adam?

DISCUSSION: Compare and contrast Adam and Jesus from this passage.

What do we have because of Jesus according to this passage?

DISCUSSION: How have you seen trials and suffering draw you closer to God and build endurance, character, and hope in your life?

ROMANS 5 NOTES

ROMANS 5 NOTES

HOW SHOULD I RESPOND?

What is the Holy Spirit asking me to do in light of this passage?

Write a prayer of honor and thanksgiving for who God is in this passage.

Because God is:

    I can:

TEACHING NOTES

TEACHING NOTES

GROUP NOTES

GROUP NOTES

BY HIS

Grace

FOR HIS

Glory

ROMANS 6

READ ROMANS 6

<u>**WHAT DOES THIS SAY?**</u>

Write a 2–3 sentence summary of this passage.

Who? What? Where? When?

List any repeated words or phrases.

List any transitional words.

WHAT DOES THIS SAY ABOUT GOD?

What characteristics of God do you see in this passage?

WHAT DOES THIS MEAN?

Look up the following words in the dictionary and write out their definitions:

Sanctification:

Sin:

_____:

_____:

CROSS-REFERENCES

John 11:17–27:

Acts 2:22–24:

1 Peter 2:16, 24–25:

_____:

_____:

STARTER QUESTIONS

What does our baptism represent?

DISCUSSION: Compare life in sin vs. life in Christ.

DISCUSSION: According to vv. 19–21, what is the fruit of sin? How does that compare to the fruit of living under the control of God?

DISCUSSION: If we live under God's forgiveness, what is wrong with continuing to live in sin?

ROMANS 6 NOTES

ROMANS 6 NOTES

HOW SHOULD I RESPOND?

What is the Holy Spirit asking me to do in light of this passage?

Write a prayer of honor and thanksgiving for who God is in this passage.

Because God is:

      I can:

TEACHING NOTES

TEACHING NOTES

GROUP NOTES

GROUP NOTES

ROMANS 7

READ ROMANS 7

<u>**WHAT DOES THIS SAY?**</u>

Write a 2–3 sentence summary of this passage.

Who? What? Where? When?

List any repeated words or phrases.

List any transitional words.

WHAT DOES THIS SAY ABOUT GOD?

What characteristics of God do you see in this passage?

WHAT DOES THIS MEAN?

Look up the following words in the dictionary and write out their definitions:

Holy:

Good:

_____:

_____:

ROMANS 7 NOTES

CROSS-REFERENCES

Exodus 19:3–6:

1 Peter 2:4–10:

_____:

_____:

STARTER QUESTIONS

What are the characteristics of the Law?

What does Paul say about the fruit of our flesh?

DISCUSSION: Why do we still need the Law if we are free from it?

DISCUSSION: How does the Holy Spirit help us serve in a new way?

ROMANS 7 NOTES

HOW SHOULD I RESPOND?

What is the Holy Spirit asking me to do in light of this passage?

Write a prayer of honor and thanksgiving for who God is in this passage.

Because God is:

      I can:

TEACHING NOTES

TEACHING NOTES

GROUP NOTES

GROUP NOTES

By His Grace for His Glory

ROMANS 8

READ ROMANS 8

<u>**WHAT DOES THIS SAY?**</u>

Write a 2–3 sentence summary of this passage.

Who? What? Where? When?

List any repeated words or phrases.

List any transitional words.

WHAT DOES THIS SAY ABOUT GOD?

What characteristics of God do you see in this passage?

WHAT DOES THIS MEAN?

Look up the following words in the dictionary and write out their definitions:

Intercede:

Condemn:

Adopt:

_____:

_____:

CROSS-REFERENCES

John 3:16–17:

1 Thessalonians 4:3–4:

Psalm 44:22:

_____ :

_____ :

STARTER QUESTIONS

DISCUSSION: Read Romans 8:1–3 and John 3:16–17. What does it mean to "not be condemned"? What is the result of Jesus coming?

What are the benefits of being controlled by the Spirit? What are the results of being controlled by the flesh?

Who intercedes for us? What does this mean?

DISCUSSION: What does it mean to be "more than conquerors"?

ROMANS 8 NOTES

ROMANS 8 NOTES

HOW SHOULD I RESPOND?

What is the Holy Spirit asking me to do in light of this passage?

Write a prayer of honor and thanksgiving for who God is in this passage.

Because God is:

     I can:

TEACHING NOTES

TEACHING NOTES

GROUP NOTES

GROUP NOTES

BY HIS

Grace

FOR HIS

Glory

ROMANS 9

READ ROMANS 9

WHAT DOES THIS SAY?

Write a 2–3 sentence summary of this passage.

Who? What? Where? When?

List any repeated words or phrases.

List any transitional words.

WHAT DOES THIS SAY ABOUT GOD?

What characteristics of God do you see in this passage?

WHAT DOES THIS MEAN?

Look up the following words in the dictionary and write out their definitions:

Sovereign:

Mercy:

_____:

_____:

ROMANS 9 NOTES

CROSS-REFERENCES

Exodus 9:13–17:

2 Peter 3:9:

_____:

_____:

STARTER QUESTIONS

What do you know about:

Abraham and Sarah?

Isaac and Rebekah?

Jacob and Esau?

What is confusing about this passage? What questions do you have?

DISCUSSION: How do these quoted verses help explain this passage?

Genesis 21:12

Genesis 18:10

Genesis 25:23

Malachi 1:2–3

Exodus 33:19

Exodus 9:16

Hosea 2:23

Hosea 1:10

Isaiah 10:22–23

Isaiah 1:9

Isaiah 28:16

DISCUSSION: What is true of God in this passage?

ROMANS 9 NOTES

ROMANS 9 NOTES

HOW SHOULD I RESPOND?

What is the Holy Spirit asking me to do in light of this passage?

Write a prayer of honor and thanksgiving for who God is in this passage.

Because God is:

    I can:

TEACHING NOTES

TEACHING NOTES

GROUP NOTES

GROUP NOTES

By His Grace For His Glory

ROMANS 10

READ ROMANS 10

WHAT DOES THIS SAY?

Write a 2–3 sentence summary of this passage.

Who? What? Where? When?

List any repeated words or phrases.

List any transitional words.

WHAT DOES THIS SAY ABOUT GOD?

What characteristics of God do you see in this passage?

WHAT DOES THIS MEAN?

Look up the following words in the dictionary and write out their definitions:

You may want to revisit the definitions for righteousness (Chapter 2), justified (Chapter 3), and faith (Chapter 3).

Shame:

Believe:

_____:

_____:

CROSS-REFERENCES

Deuteronomy 6:4–6:

Nehemiah 9:26–31:

_____:

_____:

STARTER QUESTIONS

Paul mentions both the heart and mouth play a role in our salvation. Why is this necessary?

What does this passage tell us about who can be saved?

DISCUSSION: How do these quoted verses help explain this passage?

Deuteronomy 30:14

Joel 2:32

Isaiah 52:7

Isaiah 53:1

Psalm 19:4

Deuteronomy 32:21

Isaiah 65:1–2

DISCUSSION: What does this passage tell us about our role in the gospel?

ROMANS 10 NOTES

ROMANS 10 NOTES

HOW SHOULD I RESPOND?

What is the Holy Spirit asking me to do in light of this passage?

Write a prayer of honor and thanksgiving for who God is in this passage.

Because God is:

      I can:

TEACHING NOTES

TEACHING NOTES

GROUP NOTES

GROUP NOTES

By His Grace

For His Glory

ROMANS 11

READ ROMANS 11

WHAT DOES THIS SAY?

Write a 2–3 sentence summary of this passage.

Who? What? Where? When?

List any repeated words or phrases.

List any transitional words.

WHAT DOES THIS SAY ABOUT GOD?

What characteristics of God do you see in this passage?

WHAT DOES THIS MEAN?

Look up the following words in the dictionary and write out their definitions:

Jealous:

Graft:

_____:

_____:

CROSS-REFERENCES

Hosea 14:1–9:

Ezekiel 36:24–32:

James 3:14:

_____:

_____:

STARTER QUESTIONS

How does Paul describe the family of God in this passage?

DISCUSSION: How do these quoted verses help explain this passage?

1 Kings 19:10, 14

1 Kings 19:18

Psalm 69:22–23

Isaiah 59:20–21

BONUS: Do an internet search on grafting olive trees. How does the insight gained better explain this passage?

DISCUSSION: Paul ends this section in vv. 33–36 with praise for who God is. Why is this a fitting end to a difficult section of Scripture?

HOW SHOULD I RESPOND?

What is the Holy Spirit asking me to do in light of this passage?

Write a prayer of honor and thanksgiving for who God is in this passage.

Because God is:

    I can:

154

TEACHING NOTES

TEACHING NOTES

GROUP NOTES

GROUP NOTES

BY HIS

Grace

FOR HIS

Glory

ROMANS 12

READ ROMANS 12

WHAT DOES THIS SAY?

Write a 2–3 sentence summary of this passage.

Who? What? Where? When?

List any repeated words or phrases.

List any transitional words.

WHAT DOES THIS SAY ABOUT GOD?

What characteristics of God do you see in this passage?

WHAT DOES THIS MEAN?

Look up the following words in the dictionary and write out their definitions:

Conform:

Renew:

_____:

_____:

CROSS-REFERENCES

1 Thessalonians 4:3–8:

1 Peter 1:13–21:

Deuteronomy 32:35:

Proverbs 25:21–22:

_____:

_____:

STARTER QUESTIONS

What is God's will?

DISCUSSION: How do we renew our minds?

DISCUSSION: What are the characteristics of the Church, the body of Christ?

Why does renewing our mind and knowing God's will come before the list of characteristics of the church?

ROMANS 12 NOTES

ROMANS 12 NOTES

HOW SHOULD I RESPOND?

What is the Holy Spirit asking me to do in light of this passage?

Write a prayer of honor and thanksgiving for who God is in this passage.

Because God is:

    I can:

TEACHING NOTES

TEACHING NOTES

GROUP NOTES

GROUP NOTES

BY HIS

Grace

FOR HIS

Glory

ROMANS 13

READ ROMANS 13
WHAT DOES THIS SAY?

Write a 2–3 sentence summary of this passage.

Who? What? Where? When?

List any repeated words or phrases.

List any transitional words.

WHAT DOES THIS SAY ABOUT GOD?

What characteristics of God do you see in this passage?

WHAT DOES THIS MEAN?

Look up the following words in the dictionary and write out their definitions:

Submit:

Authority:

_____:

_____:

CROSS-REFERENCES

Hebrews 13:17:

Leviticus 19:9–18:

Matthew 22:34–40:

_____:

_____:

STARTER QUESTIONS

CONTEXT: What do you know about the Roman government during this time?

DISCUSSION: How are we able to walk in light and not darkness? What does that mean for our ability to do as Paul commands in this passage?

What does it mean to "make no provision for the flesh"?

DISCUSSION: What are some practical ways we can "put on Jesus"?

ROMANS 13 NOTES

ROMANS 13 NOTES

HOW SHOULD I RESPOND?

What is the Holy Spirit asking me to do in light of this passage?

Write a prayer of honor and thanksgiving for who God is in this passage.

Because God is:

    I can:

TEACHING NOTES

TEACHING NOTES

GROUP NOTES

BY HIS

Grace

FOR HIS

Glory

ROMANS 14

READ ROMANS 14

<u>**WHAT DOES THIS SAY?**</u>

Write a 2–3 sentence summary of this passage.

Who? What? Where? When?

List any repeated words or phrases.

List any transitional words.

WHAT DOES THIS SAY ABOUT GOD?

What characteristics of God do you see in this passage?

WHAT DOES THIS MEAN?

Look up the following words in the dictionary and write out their definitions:

Judgment:

Pride:

_____:

_____:

CROSS-REFERENCES

Isaiah 45:18–25: _____

_____

Leviticus 11: _____

_____

Acts 10:9–33: _____

_____

_____: _____

_____

_____: _____

_____

STARTER QUESTIONS

What do you know of the differences in the diets of Jews versus Gentiles? (see cross-references)

DISCUSSION: What are the marks of the kingdom of God? How do we respond to one another in light of these characteristics?

DISCUSSION: What is our purpose within the Church, the body of Christ? How does this reflect the character of God?

ROMANS 14 NOTES

HOW SHOULD I RESPOND?

What is the Holy Spirit asking me to do in light of this passage?

Write a prayer of honor and thanksgiving for who God is in this passage.

Because God is:

    I can:

190

TEACHING NOTES

TEACHING NOTES

GROUP NOTES

GROUP NOTES

By His Grace For His Glory

ROMANS 15

READ ROMANS 15

<u>**WHAT DOES THIS SAY?**</u>

Write a 2–3 sentence summary of this passage.

Who? What? Where? When?

List any repeated words or phrases.

List any transitional words.

WHAT DOES THIS SAY ABOUT GOD?

What characteristics of God do you see in this passage?

WHAT DOES THIS MEAN?

Look up the following words in the dictionary and write out their definitions:

Glory:

Harmony:

_____:

_____:

CROSS-REFERENCES

Romans 5:1–5:

Philippians 2:1–11:

_____:

_____:

STARTER QUESTIONS

What does the Word of God provide for us? What does this tell us about the importance of studying Scripture?

DISCUSSION: How do these quoted verses help explain this passage?

Psalm 69:9

2 Samuel 22:50

Psalm 18:49 (read the whole Psalm; it's a good one!)

Deuteronomy 32:43

Psalm 117:1

Isaiah 11:10

Isaiah 52:15

DISCUSSION: What does it mean to welcome or accept one another?

What is hope? Why do you think Paul ends the main part of his letter with hope?

ROMANS 15 NOTES

ROMANS 15 NOTES

<u>HOW SHOULD I RESPOND?</u>

What is the Holy Spirit asking me to do in light of this passage?

Write a prayer of honor and thanksgiving for who God is in this passage.

Because God is:

    I can:

TEACHING NOTES

TEACHING NOTES

GROUP NOTES

GROUP NOTES

BY HIS
Grace
FOR HIS
Glory

ROMANS 16

ROMANS 16 NOTES

READ ROMANS 16

<u>**WHAT DOES THIS SAY?**</u>

Write a 2–3 sentence summary of this passage.

Who? What? Where? When?

List any repeated words or phrases.

List any transitional words.

WHAT DOES THIS SAY ABOUT GOD?

What characteristics of God do you see in this passage?

WHAT DOES THIS MEAN?

Look up the following words in the dictionary and write out their definitions:

Peace:

Obstacle:

_____:

_____:

CROSS-REFERENCES

Acts 18:2:

Genesis 3:15:

_____:

_____:

STARTER QUESTIONS

Look at the list of names. What other Scriptures give further explanation to who some of these people were? How many men? Women? What were their occupations? How did they serve the church?

DISCUSSION: What warning does Paul give in his closing verses?

Write out vv. 25–27.

DISCUSSION: How has studying Romans changed you?

DISCUSSION: What do you now know about God that you didn't before?

DISCUSSION: What truths will stick with you?

ROMANS 16 NOTES

ROMANS 16 NOTES

HOW SHOULD I RESPOND?

What is the Holy Spirit asking me to do in light of this passage?

Write a prayer of honor and thanksgiving for who God is in this passage.

Because God is:

I can:

TEACHING NOTES

TEACHING NOTES

GROUP NOTES

GROUP NOTES

BY HIS Grace FOR HIS Glory

ADDITIONAL NOTES

VERSES ABOUT GRACE

ADDITIONAL NOTES

VERSES ABOUT GOD'S GLORY

QUOTED OLD TESTAMENT VERSES

ADDITIONAL NOTES

ADDITIONAL NOTES

feasting at the table

It's no secret that I *love* tacos. I do not know where my obsession began, but there's just something about little tortillas stuffed with all kinds of deliciousness that screams party and fun every time I eat them. You know what goes well with tacos? Queso! Ooey gooey yummy cheesy goodness—either on the side with chips or on the taco. But our family's absolute favorite way to enjoy queso on taco night is on double-stack cheesy tacos: take a flour tortilla, spread queso all over one side, and then wrap it around a hard-shell taco. You're welcome.

This isn't necessarily an "authentic" queso recipe, but I love the flavor and that it's homemade. Best of all, it's super easy and super fast! The mild flavor of the Monterey Jack cheese provides a silky background that allows the spices to pop. You'll want to buy a block of cheese and shred it yourself. Commercially shredded cheese is tossed in anti-caking powders, and it will prevent your queso from becoming smooth. This recipe calls for fire-roasted tomatoes, which adds a smokiness to the queso. You can use regular canned diced tomatoes if you can't find fire roasted. Lastly, if you don't want to buy and measure out all the different spices, you can use 2 teaspoons of your favorite taco seasoning in place of the spices. If you choose to go that route, you probably won't need to add any salt as most taco seasonings already have salt in them.

I typically make my own seasoning mix so I can control the amounts and quality of the ingredients. Here's a little bonus tip: in this recipe, you'll find two of my go-to spices: granulated garlic and granulated onion. This is different than garlic or onion powders in that it packs more flavor. It's actually tiny, coarse, dehydrated pieces of onion and garlic. I sprinkle a little of both on almost everything I make: rice, roasted broccoli, roasted Brussels sprouts, (or any roasted veggie for that matter!), burgers, etc. It really elevates the flavor without being overpowering. You can find both at specialty online spice stores. (I know that sounds fancy, but it's not much more expensive because you are buying in bulk. In fact, I typically buy large amounts of all my spices from these stores. It ends up being cheaper than buying packets of taco seasoning.)

If you happen to have leftovers of the queso, this recipe reheats well! Just put it in a microwave-safe bowl and reheat in 30-second increments, stirring between each interval, until warm and smooth. I hope you enjoy this addition to your Taco Tuesday. Oh, who are we kidding? Every night should be taco night!

Happy feasting!

ERIN'S EASY QUESO

Time: 15 minutes
Yield: about 3 cups

INGREDIENTS

1 (8 ounce) block Monterey Jack cheese
1 tablespoon cornstarch
½ teaspoon chili powder
½ teaspoon cumin
½ teaspoon granulated onion
¼ teaspoon paprika
¼ teaspoon coriander
¼ teaspoon granulated garlic

1 (12 ounce) can evaporated milk
1 (4 ounce) can chopped green chilis
½ cup fire roasted diced tomatoes (preferably no salt added)

Kosher salt

INSTRUCTIONS

1. Shred the cheese and place in a medium sized bowl.
2. To the cheese, add the cornstarch and the next six ingredients. Toss to coat the cheese.
3. In a medium saucepan over medium heat, mix the evaporated milk, green chilis, and diced tomatoes. (If you want smaller pieces of tomato, I crush mine by hand as I add them to the pan.)
4. Stir the mixture frequently to prevent the milk from scalding.
5. Once hot, add the cheese and spices and stir until the cheese is melted and the mixture is smooth. Add salt to taste (you shouldn't need much). Keep warm until ready to serve.
6. Serve with your favorite tortilla chips, tortillas, or even vegetables.

about Erin

ERIN H. WARREN is passionate about equipping and encouraging women to discover God's truths for themselves. She is the author of *Feasting on Truth: Savor the Life-giving Word of God*, leads and teaches Bible study through her ministry Feasting on Truth, and has published several Bible studies. She and her husband, Kris, have three littles (who aren't so little anymore), and they live in Central Florida. She loves a house full of people and a table full of food and hopes tacos never go out of style. You can find more information about Feasting on Truth on her website: FeastingOnTruth.com. You can also connect with her on Instagram: @erinhwarren and @feastingontruth and YouTube: www.youtube.com/c/erinhwarren.

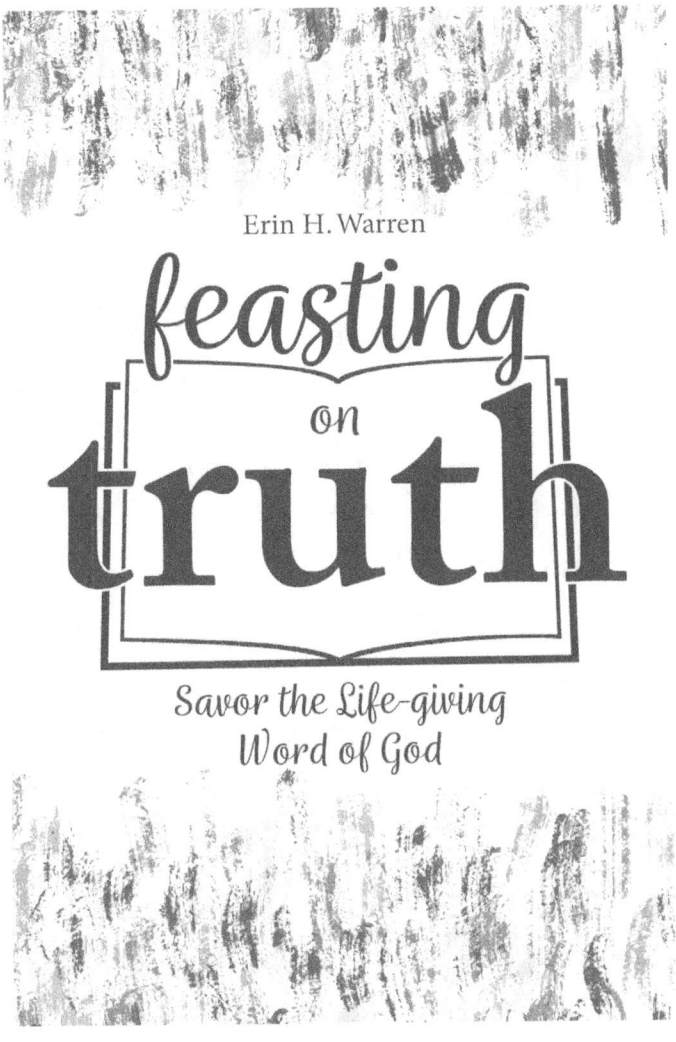

Erin H. Warren

feasting

on

truth

Savor the Life-giving Word of God

FEASTING ON TRUTH

SAVOR THE LIFE-GIVING WORD OF GOD

The Word of God is our very life, but Erin Warren felt anything but alive. Her husband was sick. Her world was falling apart, and she had questions. Feel-good faith was not enough; she needed deep, sustaining truths.

Through her own wrestling, Erin Warren addresses the obstacles that held her back when it came to Bible study and how she discovered to savor the life-giving Word of God.

The word *feast* is rooted in abundance. That is what awaits us in the pages of Scripture: a table laid out before us, not only for our essential nourishment, but for our enjoyment.

FeastingOnTruth.com/Books

STORIES FROM THE WILDERNESS

A STUDY OF THE ISRAELITES' JOURNEY FROM EGYPT TO THE PROMISED LAND

The wilderness. It is a place that feels hard, empty, lifeless, and pathless, and it often leaves us with questions about who God is. But where we see a place that is worthless, confusing, and chaotic, God sees a place to display His power. Time and time again throughout Scripture, God takes the worthless, seemingly wasteful, confusing, chaotic, and empty places and uses them as a backdrop to prove His character, draw us in, and display His glory.

FeastingOnTruth.com/Wilderness

TO DWELL IN OUR MIDST

A STUDY OF THE TABERNACLE AND HOW IT POINTS US TO JESUS

Why study this ancient tent? What does knowing about the Tabernacle have to do with our faith on this side of the cross? Everything. This tent is not merely ritual or history or good information—it's essential to understanding our salvation. Our detailed and deliberate God gave us the Tabernacle because one day, He would give us Jesus. It's an invitation into a relationship with our Holy God. Discover God's plan to dwell in our midst through Jesus Christ.

FeastingOnTruth.com/Dwell

WAYMAKER

AN ADVENT STUDY THROUGH THE BOOK OF HEBREWS

Jesus' coming was more than giving us forgiveness of sins or to part the way before us. He came to part the divide between God and us, between us and heaven. Jesus is the One who made a way to a restored relationship with God. No other book gives us a more comprehensive view of Jesus as our Way Maker than the book of Hebrews.

FeastingOnTruth.com/WayMaker

LIGHT AND LIFE

AN INDUCTIVE BIBLE STUDY ON PSALM 119

We hear it all the time: we need to read the Bible every day. But why is it so important that we know, understand, and apply this ancient book to our lives today? What's in it for us? In Psalm 119, we see over and over that God's Word brings life, and it's a light to guide us. If we truly knew the power the Word of God has in our lives, we wouldn't be able to put it down.

FeastingOnTruth.com/LightAndLife

UNEXPECTED SAVIOR

AN INDUCTIVE BIBLE STUDY ON THE GOSPEL OF MARK

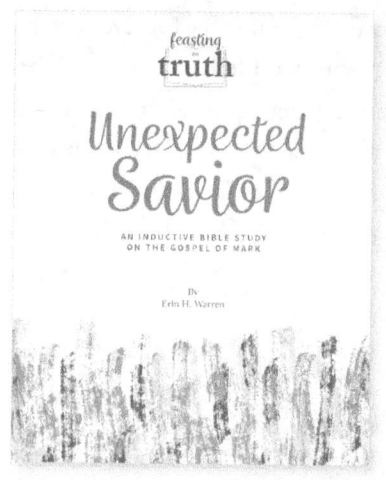

The Gospel of Mark challenges the expected ideal of the Messiah—not a conquering king or a wish-granting genie, but rather a man of sorrows and a suffering servant. This short yet impactful account of Jesus' life reveals the character of the One who came to save us. Jesus mourned the brokenness around Him: the sickness, the pain, the hardness of heart. He grew angry at the sin of those who led His sheep astray. He was the One who came not to be served, but to serve. He came to prove the faithfulness of God and provide unshakeable hope as we walk through hardships.

FeastingOnTruth.com/Mark